21st
Century
Junior
Library

FARM ANIMALS
HORSES

by Cecilia Minden

CHERRY LAKE PUBLISHING * ANN ARBOR, MICHIGAN

CHERRY
LAKE
Publishing

Published in the United States of America by Cherry Lake Publishing
Ann Arbor, Michigan
www.cherrylakepublishing.com

Content Adviser: Laurie Rincker, Assistant Professor of Agriculture, Eastern Kentucky University

Photo Credits: Cover and page 4 and 6, ©Condor 36, used under license from Shutterstock, Inc.;
cover and page 8, ©iStockphoto.com/DaydreamsGirl; page 10, ©iStockphoto.com/RhondaSuka;
page 12, ©Margo Harrison, used under license from Shutterstock, Inc.; cover and page 14,
©LesPalenik, used under license from Shutterstock, Inc.; page 16, ©Bill Gruber, used under license
from Shutterstock, Inc.; page 18, ©iStockphoto.com/inshot; page 20, ©Gordon Swanson, used
under license from Shutterstock, Inc.

LIBRARY OF CONGRESS CATALOGING-IN-PUBLICATION DATA
Minden, Cecilia.
 Farm animals: Horses / by Cecilia Minden.
   p. cm.—(21st century junior library)
 Includes index.
 ISBN-13: 978-1-60279-541-9
 ISBN-10: 1-60279-541-X
 1. Horses—Juvenile literature. I. Title. II. Title: Horses. III. Series.
 SF302.M56 2010
 636.1—dc22   2009003314

Cherry Lake Publishing would like to acknowledge the work of
The Partnership for 21st Century Skills.
Please visit www.21stcenturyskills.org for more information.

CONTENTS

Horses need room to run.

Who Says Neigh?

What do you think of when you hear the word *horse*? Do you think of a pony racing across a field? Do you think of horses pulling wagons? Let's "ride on" to the next page. There is a lot to learn about horses. They are amazing animals!

Foals are much smaller than their mothers.

Horse Facts

A baby horse is called a **foal**. Foals are usually born in the spring. At birth, the foal weighs about 100 pounds (45.4 kilograms). Fully grown horses can weigh more than 1,000 pounds (453.6 kg). Horses have adult teeth by the time they are 5 years old.

There are many different kinds of horses.

A **yearling** is a horse between 1 and 2 years old. Males under age 4 are **colts**. A young female is a **filly**. Females more than 4 years old are **mares**. Males more than 4 years old are **stallions**.

Ask Questions!

There are many horse **breeds**. Different breeds come in different sizes and colors. Some breeds are used for racing. Other breeds are used on farms. Do you know any horse owners? What is their favorite breed? Asking questions helps you learn more about horses.

Feeding a horse is a good way to make a
new friend.

Horses can live to be 30 years old. They like to eat grass or hay. Horses need a lot of water, too. They drink 10 to 12 gallons (38 to 45 liters) of water every day! Horses also like treats. Apples are a favorite snack.

Think!

Horses have special teeth. The ones in the front have sharp edges. The teeth in the back are wide. They have a flat but rough surface. Think about the shape of these teeth. How might they help a horse eat its food?

Some farmers still like to use horses to pull
their plows.

Horses on the Farm

Long ago, it was hard to run a farm without a horse. Horses were used to help clear the land for planting. They could pull up big rocks and tree stumps. Horses pulled the **plow** so a farmer could plant crops.

Some farmers offer horse-drawn wagon rides
to visitors.

Horses were also used to bring in the crops. They pulled machines that cut down plants. Crops were loaded onto a wagon. The horses pulled the wagons into town. There the farmer could sell his crops. He used the money to buy things for his farm. The horse-drawn wagon carried everything back home.

Horseback riding with a group of friends is fun!

Today, horses aren't used as much as they were in the past. Most farmers use machines that run on fuel. Trucks are used to haul crops.

Horses can bring in extra income, however. Farmers rent their horses to people who like to ride. They also rent carriages. Hayrides are a popular pastime in the fall.

Look!

Take a good look at a horse's head. Where are its eyes? You might notice that a horse's eyes are spaced far apart. In fact, they are on the sides of its head. How might this help a horse stay safe?

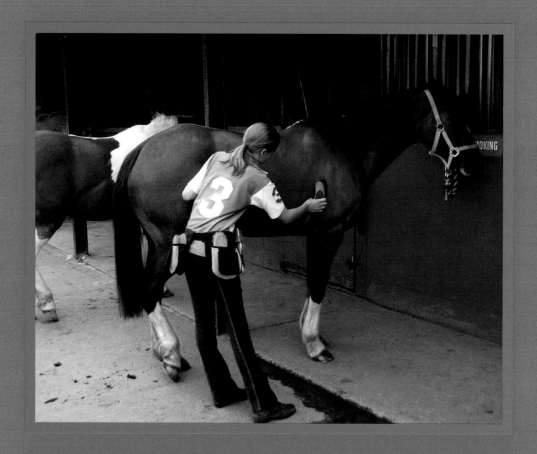

Many horses enjoy being brushed.

Caring for Horses

Caring for a horse is a big job. Horses need shelter from bad weather. They need land for running and **grazing**.

Caring for a horse also means keeping its coat healthy. It must be washed and brushed. A **farrier** has a special job. He or she keeps a horse's hooves in top shape.

Riding lessons are a good way to learn more about horses.

Would you like to ride a horse?
Maybe a place near your home offers
riding lessons. Check it out. With a lot of
practice, you could become a great rider
someday. Giddyup!

Make a Guess!

Guess how tall the smallest horse breeds are. Guess how much they weigh. How about the largest horse breeds? You might be able to find the answers online. The library is a good place to look, too. Were your guesses correct?

GLOSSARY

breeds (BREEDZ) specific types or kinds of animals

colts (KOHLTSS) male horses that are less than 4 years old

farrier (FAIR-ee-yur) a person who makes horseshoes and fits them onto horses

filly (FIL-ee) a female horse that is less than 4 years old

foal (FOHL) a horse that is less than 1 year old

grazing (GRAY-zeeng) eating grass that is growing in a field

mares (MAIRZ) female horses that are more than 4 years old

plow (PLOU) a piece of farm equipment used to turn over soil before planting crops

stallions (STAL-yuhnz) male horses that are more than 4 years old

yearling (YIHR-leeng) a horse that is between 1 and 2 years old

FIND OUT MORE

BOOKS

Doyle, Malachy, and Angelo Rinaldi (illustrator). *Horse*. New York: Margaret K. McElderry Books, 2008.

Simon, Seymour. *Horses*. New York: HarperCollins Publishers, 2006.

WEB SITES

Animal Planet: Tour a Horse

animal.discovery.com/guides/ horses/tour/horsetour/horsetour.html
Learn more about the parts of a horse's body

Circle R Ranch—Fun Horse Facts

www.circlerranch.com/education/ edu4.html
Find interesting facts about horses

INDEX

ABOUT THE AUTHOR

Cecilia Minden, PhD, is a literacy consultant and author of many books for children. She lives with her family near Chapel Hill, North Carolina. Dr. Minden recommends that you explore the library to find many fiction books about horses.